WITHDRAWN

WHO'LL SAVE THE PLOWBOY?

Who'll Save the Plowboy?

A new play by
FRANK D. GILROY

RANDOM HOUSE
NEW YORK

FIRST PRINTING

© COPYRIGHT, AS AN UNPUBLISHED WORK, 1959, BY
FRANK D. GILROY

© COPYRIGHT, 1962, BY FRANK D. GILROY

Photographs by courtesy of Henry Grossman

Library of Congress Catalog Card Number: 62–17160

Manufactured in the United States of America

For RUTH

WHO'LL SAVE THE PLOWBOY? *was first presented by T. Edward Hambleton and Norris Houghton at the Phoenix Theatre, New York City, on January 9, 1962, with the following cast:*

(IN ORDER OF APPEARANCE)

ALBERT COBB	Gerald O'Loughlin
HELEN COBB	Rebecca Darke
LARRY DOYLE	William Smithers
DOCTOR	Burton Mallory
MRS. DOYLE	Dorothy Peterson
THE MAN	Tom Sawyer
THE BOY	Patrick O'Shaughnessy

Directed by Daniel Petrie

Costumes and scenery by Norris Houghton

Lighting by John Robertson

SYNOPSIS

The scene is New York City. The time, the Present.

ACT ONE

SCENE ONE. Two days before Christmas. Evening.
SCENE TWO. One hour later.

ACT TWO

The following morning.

ACT ONE

Place: The scene is a lower-middle-class apartment in New York. The living room occupies the central area of the stage. Windows open on a courtyard four floors below. A swinging door leads off to the kitchen. French doors, covered with curtains, lead to a bedroom. At stage left is a passage to the bathroom and another bedroom, neither of which are seen. At stage right the living room leads to a foyer. A door in the foyer opens on the hallway outside. When the door is open, a part of this hallway is visible, including stairs leading from the floor above and the head of the stairs leading from the floor below. There is an upright piano in the living room. Its keyboard is covered. There is a phone on a stand in the foyer.

It is about nine P.M., two days before Christmas, of the present year.

At rise, ALBERT COBB, *thirty-five, a large man of strong build, who has gone a bit to seed, dressed in his best clothes, bounces around the room in an attitude of happy expectation. He sips from a beer can, whistles snatches of "I've Got Sixpence," and chuckles at some private memory.* HELEN COBB, *thirty-five, his wife, plain in appearance, is darning socks. Through a partly open window comes a muted tangle of city noises.*

ALBERT   What time is it now?

HELEN   Nine fifteen.
     (ALBERT *paces a bit more*)

3

ALBERT   What time is it?

HELEN   Nine sixteen.

ALBERT   Why don't he get here? (ALBERT *continues to pace, stops, laughs*) Me lying in the dark bleeding to death and listening. And everything so still I could hear every word they said.

HELEN   I wish you'd cut your toenails once in a while.

ALBERT   "Who'll save the Plowboy?" says the Lieutenant. . . . For a long time nobody said a word and you couldn't blame them: The Germans were using me as bait. "You still with us, Plowboy?" the Lieutenant shouts. "Well, I could have been a hero by making out I was dead. But who'd have given me credit for it?

HELEN   When was the last time you cut your toenails?

ALBERT   "I'm still here," I said back. "But I won't be much longer." And then Larry spoke up: "Hang on, Plowboy, I'm coming for you," he yells. There was a whole lot of voices after that. I couldn't make it all out but I knew they were trying to talk him out of it. Telling him he was committing suicide. But he did it. They threw everything at him. He was hit before he got to me. He had to carry me piggyback and I could feel the blood running down his side. I passed out before we got there, but we made it. A miracle. That's what everyone said it was: a miracle.

HELEN   These don't look like your socks.

ALBERT   Did you get more beer?

HELEN   Yes. (*Holds up a pair of socks*) Where did these socks come from?

ALBERT   How do I know? . . . How much beer did you get?

HELEN   Twelve cans.

ALBERT   He was always a great one for beer . . . or anything with alcohol, for that matter.

HELEN   It's how many years since you saw him?

ALBERT   Fifteen. . . . I'd like to have a nickel for every time I carried him back to the barracks drunk as a coot. I'd be a millionaire.

HELEN   And vice versa I'm sure.

ALBERT   I didn't drink in those days.

HELEN   I believe that.

ALBERT   It's the truth. Not a drop. He'll tell you.

HELEN   If he ever gets here. You sure he said tonight?

ALBERT   Yes. Chances are he got lost. It's the first time he's been to New York.

HELEN How do you know?

ALBERT If he'd been here before, he'd have looked me up. . . .
We were like brothers.

HELEN So you've told me. How long is he going to be in New
York?

ALBERT Just overnight. God, but he was a crazy galoot. Always raising some sort of hell. And comical . . .

HELEN If you were so close, how come he stopped writing
to you? How come your letters came back "address un-
known"?

ALBERT You seem bound to plant a suspicion in my mind.
Well, it won't work.

HELEN Only persons I know who don't have forwarding ad-
dresses are people trying to run away from something.

ALBERT Wait till you see how skinny he is alongside of me.
You won't believe that he was able to lift me, much less
carry me as far as he did. . . . Of course I wasn't quite so
heavy then.

HELEN I don't like it. No word in years and then suddenly
he pops up. . . . He wants something.

ALBERT Whatever he wants that I can give him he's en-
titled to.

HELEN Whatever you can give him is very little and half mine. So don't be too generous.

ALBERT How could I be too generous to a man who risked his life to save mine? And what makes you sure he wants something? Isn't it possible he might just want to see me for old times' sake?

HELEN Don't be disappointed when he tries to sell you an insurance policy.

ALBERT He's not like that.

HELEN People change.

ALBERT He couldn't change that much. . . . You know something—you sound like you're mad at him.

HELEN I don't even know him. Why should I be mad?

ALBERT You sound like you are. (*He takes a swallow of beer as a short figure played on a trumpet sounds through the window. The figure is repeated as an exercise in various keys. At the first sound* HELEN *is transfixed; listens*) That's the first time I heard Gabriel in weeks.

HELEN The super told me he's been touring the country with one of the big symphony orchestras.

ALBERT Too bad.

HELEN   What's too bad?

ALBERT   I was hoping he moved.

HELEN   All the noise that comes floating through that window and you object to a little music?

ALBERT   I don't hear the other noises. I'm used to them.

HELEN   You like peace and quiet so good, why don't you move to a farm, Plowboy?

ALBERT   Let's not start that.

HELEN   Well, isn't that what they used to call you . . . Plowboy?

ALBERT   Helen, I'm in a good mood. I want to be that way when *he* gets here.

HELEN   Then don't complain about a little music.

ALBERT   If he'd play a song I wouldn't mind, but all he does is . . .
   (*Parodies the trumpet figure*)

HELEN   To me it's a pleasure just to hear someone trying to improve himself at anything.

ALBERT   I guess there's another little dig at me in there some place, but I'm going to ignore it because I want to be in a good mood when Larry gets here.

8

HELEN   Keep lapping that beer and you won't even be conscious.

ALBERT   Don't worry about me. . . . What time is it?

HELEN   Nine twenty.

ALBERT   I wonder what the devil's taking him so long. (*Goes to the window, shouts in the direction of the trumpet*) Shut up!

HELEN   Maybe he changed his mind.

ALBERT   That's what you're wishing.

HELEN   I guess so.

ALBERT   Why?

HELEN   I can't see any good coming out of it.

ALBERT   You know who you sound like when you talk gloomy like this: your mother. Old moaning low. Old laugh in the morning and cry at night. That's just who you sound like. Well, go ahead, talk all you want. You won't get a rise out of me. Not tonight.

HELEN   Why not? Just what's so special about tonight?

ALBERT   I'll tell you: My friend . . . the only real friend I ever had . . . the only one . . . he's coming to see me and I'm looking forward to it . . . I haven't looked forward to anything

9

else in years. . . . But I'm looking forward to seeing my friend and you're not going to spoil it. . . . You never met him but you hate him. I asked you why, but do you think I'm so stupid that I don't know why. . . . Well, tonight you're going to keep your mouth shut. . . . You're going to make him feel welcome . . . like this was a happy house he came to.

HELEN   And the boy? What do we say about the boy?

ALBERT   Nothing.

HELEN   He'll ask.

ALBERT   We'll say he's visiting relatives.

HELEN   No.

ALBERT   *Yes* . . . I won't ruin his evening. . . . We'll say the boy is visiting relatives upstate.

HELEN   The day after tomorrow is Christmas. Kids usually spend Christmas with their parents.

ALBERT   All right. He'll be home for Christmas. Now let's drop it . . . I feel lousy. I hope you're satisfied. (*Goes to the window and shouts up toward the trumpet sounds*) Shut up that lousy horn! (*Slams the window shut. The trumpet can't be heard*) The simplest thing: a friend is coming to visit. Why can't he just come without everything getting mixed up?

Gerald O'Loughlin and Rebecca Darke
as ALBERT COBB and HELEN COBB

HELEN   I'd like to know where these socks came from.

ALBERT   Sometimes I think you want me to kill you.

HELEN   They're not even your size.

ALBERT   I think sometimes you purposely try to make me do that.

HELEN   Don't you have any idea where these socks came from?

ALBERT   Well, the hell with all that tonight. I'm in a good mood and I'm going to stay that way. What time is it now?

HELEN   Nine twenty-three.

ALBERT   God damn it, where is he? (*He goes into the kitchen and reappears almost immediately with a new can of beer which he opens*) Wouldn't it be a laugh on you and your suspicions if it turned out he came to do me a good turn. That he had some good deal he wants me in on.

HELEN   It would also be a laugh on me if Santa Claus appeared, because I don't believe in him either.

ALBERT   The fact is you don't believe in anything.

HELEN   And you?

ALBERT   I believe in Larry. I have to believe in a man who risked his life to save me . . . I have to believe in something.

HELEN I don't.

ALBERT That's the only thing I have left.

HELEN I have nothing left.

ALBERT You're jealous of me.

HELEN Green with it.

ALBERT I still have hopes. You can't stand that.

HELEN I have hopes. Want to know what they are?

ALBERT No.

HELEN Every night before I go to bed I hope I won't wake up in the morning.

ALBERT You shouldn't say things like that. Even joking.

HELEN Who's going to hear me?

ALBERT Please lay off that talk in front of Larry.

HELEN I thought you said he had a sense of humor.

ALBERT If he makes me any sort of a decent offer I'm going to take it.

HELEN Know what my other hope is?

ALBERT Even if it means moving to another part of the country.

HELEN That the landlord gives us a new stove.

ALBERT I'm only thirty-five. Today that's nothing.

HELEN Death or a new stove. I'll settle for either one. . . . What if he wants to see a picture of the kid?

ALBERT We haven't got one.

HELEN Won't he find that strange?

ALBERT It can't be helped.

HELEN And who ever saw a happy house with no decorations two days before Christmas?

ALBERT What are you getting at?

HELEN I think we ought to tell your good friend the same lie we tell everyone else.

ALBERT Why?

HELEN Because the idea of pretending this is a happy house galls me.

ALBERT Then go to the movies.

HELEN And leave you here to be taken. Oh no.

13

ALBERT   Where are the decorations we had?

HELEN   Thrown out years ago.

ALBERT   I'll tell him we do all our decorating on Christmas Eve. . . . Why don't he get here?

HELEN   He probably did. Probably got as far as the entrance, took a good sniff of this building, realized there was no pickings, and went away.

ALBERT   You weren't always so hard.

HELEN   Not if you go back far enough.

ALBERT   I remember the first time we ever went out together.

HELEN   Don't butter me up.

ALBERT   That was the first blind date I ever had.

HELEN   Blind, deaf and dumb.

ALBERT   Remember the picture we saw? *Gilda* with Rita Hayworth—

HELEN   Stop it. . . . When your good friend gets here we'll begin the game. Till then we'll be ourselves.

ALBERT   You're a puzzle to me. I swear you are. I reckon—

HELEN   *I reckon?* . . . Well, hark the Plowboy.

ALBERT   Now what?

HELEN   Now what? . . . Now I reckon; shucks; well I'll be jiggered; well I'll be tarred and feathered. And all those other cute things one expects from a Plowboy. Here they come.

ALBERT   Just what are you suggesting?

HELEN   I'm suggesting you dab a little horse manure behind your ears and your good friend won't think you've changed one bit.

ALBERT   Knock it off.

HELEN   Now who ever heard a Plowboy use words like that.

ALBERT   You sure do know how to get a fellow riled.

HELEN   Riled: Now that's better. That just drips with country. And don't forget hornswaggled and cotton picking—

ALBERT   Cut it out.

HELEN   And down the road a piece . . . and taters . . . and— (*He slaps her across the mouth. They regard each other*) pappy and mammy.

ALBERT   Are you happy now? I hope you're happy now.

HELEN   Don't forget pappy and mammy.

ALBERT Why is it that the simplest thing can't go smoothly here?
(*A bell rings*)

HELEN That's the downstairs bell.

ALBERT I was in such a good mood before. Why the devil didn't he come when he was supposed to?

HELEN Tick the button. (*He goes to the foyer and ticks the button*) And smile. It's time to play happy house.

ALBERT Don't mention the kid unless *he* does.

HELEN Remember what I said about being too generous.

ALBERT And you remember that this man saved my life. . . . If he makes me a good offer don't sound too eager. . . . (*He listens at the door*) Don't mention the farm either.

HELEN Why not?

ALBERT Because I say so.

HELEN That doesn't leave us much to talk about.

ALBERT What's taking him so long?

HELEN Maybe somebody pushed the wrong button.

ALBERT Here he comes. (*Opens the door. Calls out*) Who goes there?

16

LARRY (*From off stage*) A friend.

ALBERT Rustle your tail, friend, and be recognized. (*He goes out into the hall and waits at the head of the stairs. As he goes out,* HELEN *goes to the window, opens it, stands looking up, listening to the trumpet*) One more flight and you got 'er licked, buddy. . . . Well, listen at him wheeze and puff. Just listen. . . . Well, for crying out loud, how the hell are you?

> (LARRY DOYLE *appears. He is thirty-five, smaller than* ALBERT *and wiry, and has a lot of gray in his hair. He is neatly dressed and carries a large package. He is winded. They contemplate each other*)

LARRY What do ya say, Plowboy?
> (*Offers his hand. They shake*)

ALBERT I say you're a sight for sore eyes. What do you say?

LARRY Nothing till I catch my breath. Four flights. That's some climb.

ALBERT Well, let me look at you. . . . Well, for crying out loud you're scrawnier than ever. . . . And look at the snow on that roof. . . . And I do believe you're uglier. Now who would have thought that was possible.

LARRY Plowboy, how are you?

ALBERT Couldn't be better.
> (LARRY *jabs him in the stomach*)

LARRY   Carrying more here than you used to.

ALBERT   Blame it on the little woman. I mean, she can cook. You married?

LARRY   No.

ALBERT   Still playing the field.

LARRY   Yeah. Sorry I'm late.

ALBERT   Forget it.

LARRY   I was hoping to get here before the kid went to sleep.

ALBERT   Say, what the devil are we doing out here in the hall. Come on inside. . . . Fifteen years. My God, it don't seem possible.
(He leads LARRY *into the apartment.* HELEN *hears them coming and closes the window)*

ALBERT   Here he is, Helen.
*(*HELEN *and* LARRY *shake hands)*

HELEN   How do you do.

LARRY   Pleased to meet you.

ALBERT   For years she's been hearing about you but I think she gave up hope of ever meeting you in person. (*To her*) Right?

18

HELEN That's right. Albert's talked about you a lot.

LARRY Knowing the Plowboy you probably got a very distorted picture.

HELEN Probably.

LARRY I was hoping to get here before the kid went to sleep. I guess I didn't make it.

ALBERT He's not here. He's visiting relatives upstate.

LARRY That's too bad.

ALBERT He'll be home for Christmas. Too bad you can't stay over.

LARRY Yeah. (*Offers the package he carries to* HELEN) I brought this for him . . . trains.

ALBERT He'll get a real bang out of that. (*To* HELEN, *who eyes the package but makes no move to accept it*) Take it, dear. . . . Take it.
    (*She takes the package and puts it on the piano*)

LARRY I was afraid he might already have trains.

ALBERT No.

LARRY How about brothers and sisters. Does he have any of those?

ALBERT   Not yet but we're working on it.

HELEN   May I ask you a question?

LARRY   Sure.

HELEN   Is it true you saved Albert's life?

ALBERT   I told you it was.

HELEN   As Larry said, you distort things. I'd like to know if you distorted that.

ALBERT   (*To* LARRY)   She's very forthright. Says anything that comes into her head, no matter how embarrassing it is. It's one of the things I like about her.

HELEN   *Did* you save his life?

LARRY   Yes.

ALBERT   And risked his own to do it as I told you a thousand times. (*To* LARRY) Say, how is that wound you got?

LARRY   No trouble.

ALBERT   Good. Well, buddy, what the devil have you been up to all these years? Last I heard you were out to California going to college. Then all of a sudden my letters started coming back.

20

LARRY While I was in college I had an offer to go into business with a fellow in Florida if I accepted right away. I took it and I guess in all the rush I forgot to leave a forwarding address. On top of that I lost yours.

ALBERT Must have been a good proposition that guy put up to you.

LARRY Yes.

ALBERT What line was that in?

LARRY Real estate.

ALBERT Is that what you're doing now?

LARRY Yes.

ALBERT Real estate is supposed to be going great guns down there in Florida.

LARRY I'm not complaining.

ALBERT (*To Helen*) What did I tell you? (*To* LARRY) I told her how everyone used to say you'd be a big success in civilian life.

LARRY I didn't say I was a big success.

ALBERT You didn't have to . . .

HELEN Living in Florida, how come you don't have a tan?

LARRY   Only tourists have time for that.

HELEN   This the first time you've ever been to New York?

LARRY   Yes.

ALBERT   Where you staying?

LARRY   The Statler.

ALBERT   We could put you up here.

LARRY   Thanks, but I'm with my mother.

ALBERT   I was going to ask how she was.

LARRY   Still going strong.

ALBERT   (*To* HELEN)   I never met her but I sure felt like I knew his mother.

HELEN   You mean his *ma*, don't you, Plowboy? (*She rises*) I'll get the beer.

LARRY   No beer for me, thanks.

HELEN   Beer is all we have.

LARRY   I'll settle for a glass of water.

ALBERT   I can jump around the corner and get some rye.

LARRY I'm off the stuff.

ALBERT What?

LARRY Uh huh. For years.

ALBERT How about that? (*To* HELEN) This guy could drink any man in the outfit under the table. I mean he was the champion guzzler of them all.

HELEN So you've told me.

ALBERT What made you quit, buddy?

LARRY Wanted to retire undefeated. Now tell me about the boy. How is he?

ALBERT Fine.
    (HELEN *exits to the kitchen*)

LARRY Who does he favor?

ALBERT Hard to say. Say, you should have brought your ma along tonight.

LARRY She was tired after the trip. Do you have any pictures of him?

ALBERT Not just now. Helen's folks keep grabbing them. We're having some more taken right after the holidays.

23

LARRY   You know, I've still got the telegram you sent when he was born saying you were naming him after me. I want you to know I'm very proud of that.

ALBERT   It was the least I could do. What brings you to New York?

LARRY   Business.

ALBERT   Must be a big deal to bring you this far.

LARRY   Not really. My mother and I are on our way to Boston to spend Christmas with some aunts, so I thought I'd kill two birds. Gee, I wish I could stay over and see young Larry, but it's impossible.

ALBERT   He'll be sorry he missed you. Say, you know, it's funny you should be living in Florida. I've often thought I wouldn't mind living there myself.

LARRY   It has its advantages. How's Larry doing in school?

ALBERT   Fine. The thought of all that sunshine the year round is very appealing.

LARRY   What grade is he in?

ALBERT   Sixth. The winters here are mean and I mean mean.

LARRY   Ten years old and he's in the sixth grade?

ALBERT   What about it?

LARRY   He must be a genius.

ALBERT   They skipped him a grade.

LARRY   They must have skipped him more than one grade.

ALBERT   Buddy, can't we talk about anything but the kid. I mean you're only going to be here a little while so why don't we talk about us some.

LARRY   You're right.

ALBERT   The reason I say that is because Helen misses the kid so much when he's away even a few days that it would be better if you mentioned him as little as possible in front of her. You know how women are.

LARRY   Sure.

ALBERT   I work for the electric company. Go around reading meters. Lots of leg work but I don't mind. Good exercise. There's all kind of employee benefits and the salary is good, but still and all I wouldn't hesitate to chuck it if the right offer came along.

LARRY   Last I heard you were driving a truck.

ALBERT   No future there. Soon as I saw that I got out. I've been with the electric company ever since. Outdoors a lot of the time and practically my own boss, so there's a lot to be said for it. Also it's a good place in case of a depression. But still I'd give it up for something better.

LARRY   What about the farm?

ALBERT   What farm?

LARRY   The farm you were going to buy.

ALBERT   Did I say I was going to buy a farm?

LARRY   Did you ever stop saying it?

ALBERT   Must have been one of those daydreams.

LARRY   What? How many times did I hear how your parents brought you to the city, and how you hated it, and how someday you were going back to the country, where you belonged.

ALBERT   That's a long time ago.

LARRY   You used to have everyone in tears, describing the day you moved to the city and how you hid in the barn until they found you and dragged you into the moving van.

ALBERT   You've got a good memory.

LARRY   I can still tell you exactly what the farm your parents had looked like.

ALBERT   Is that a fact?

LARRY   That's how much you talked about it. After all you said against city living I never expected to find you here.

26

ALBERT   She must be making that beer. . . . Helen.

HELEN (*From off stage*)   Be right there.

ALBERT   Fifteen years. Does it seem like fifteen years?
(HELEN *enters carrying a tray with two beers and a glass of water. She gives the water to* LARRY)

LARRY   Thank you.
(*She gives* ALBERT *one beer and takes one herself*)

ALBERT (*Raises his glass*)   Well, buddy, here's to old times and the genuine pleasure it is to see you again.
(*Drinks deeply*)

LARRY   That's the first time I ever saw you take a drink.

ALBERT (*To* HELEN)   Ain't that what I told you? (*To* LARRY) I was telling her before I never touched a drink in those days, but she didn't believe me.

LARRY (*To* HELEN)   It's true. (*To* ALBERT) What made you start?

HELEN   I did. When he met me he was just an innocent Plowboy and I corrupted him.

ALBERT (*Forces a laugh*)   Say, you know, I'm sitting here looking at you now and wondering how you ever got into real estate. You were that dead set against going into any kind of business. (*To* HELEN) He used to rant and rave so much that some people took him for a red.

LARRY Like you said before: That's a long time ago.

ALBERT Said business wasn't a fit way for a man to spend his life. That he was going to do something more worthwhile.

LARRY Now *you're* the one with the good memory.

ALBERT A doctor! That's what it was. (*To* HELEN) He used to get drunk as a skunk and run around waking everyone up to tell them he had decided to become a doctor. And would they please stick out their tongues and say ah.

HELEN (*To* LARRY) Why didn't you?

LARRY Become a doctor?

HELEN Yes.

LARRY I'm afraid it was just a gag.

ALBERT Gag, hell. It's what you were studying at college. I remember your letters . . . what happened, buddy? Why'd you quit?

LARRY I told you: This fellow in Florida made me an offer that was too good to turn down. On top of that I found out I wasn't as interested in medicine as I thought. That's all there is to it.

ALBERT Well, I think you did the right thing. There's a lot more money in real estate and it's not so depressing.

LARRY   True.

ALBERT   Besides, doctors never get any time off.

LARRY   Also true. Who plays the piano?

ALBERT   Helen used to but she hasn't touched it in years. Hey, do *you* still play?

LARRY   Not in a long time.

ALBERT   (*To* HELEN)   He used to be good at that ragtime stuff. (*To* LARRY)   Why don't you give us a sample?

HELEN   No ... it's out of tune and the keys are filthy.

ALBERT   I'll wipe them off.

LARRY   I'd rather talk.

ALBERT   You're the boss.

LARRY   Does young Larry show any interest in music?

ALBERT   Not much.

LARRY   Don't tell me he's tone deaf like you?

ALBERT   Yes. You sure you don't want a beer?

LARRY   Positive.

ALBERT   Well, I'm gonna put a head on this one. (*To* HELEN)
Can I get you one, dear?

HELEN   No. I have a bit of a headache. I'm going to bed soon.

ALBERT   Be right back.
> (*He exits.* LARRY *and* HELEN *regard each other; she impassively, he uneasily. He attempts to draw her into conversation*)

LARRY   One of the funniest things I can remember is your
husband trying to carry a tune . . . (*He chuckles but elicits
no response or change of expression from her*) I bet I called
a dozen A. Cobbs before I got the Plowboy. Thought sure
I'd recognize his voice right away but I didn't.

HELEN   Common.

LARRY   What's that?

HELEN   The name Cobb. My maiden name—there was only
one in the whole Manhattan book.
> (*Silence*)

LARRY   Albert tells me the boy is already in the sixth grade.
Sounds like you have a quiz kid on your hands. . . . (*No
response*) I was saying to Albert that I never expected to
reach you people here.

HELEN   Why?

30

LARRY   Because all he used to talk about was buying a farm and getting out of the city.

HELEN   We talk a lot while the day is long.

LARRY   The farm was more than talk and he hated the city. Why is he still here?

HELEN   You hated business. Why are you in real estate?
(ALBERT *reënters the room carrying a full glass of beer*)

ALBERT   In your honor I had Helen get another dozen cans. But I don't guess they'll go to waste. (*Drinks*) You know it's a shame you didn't call earlier. You could have come for dinner. Helen's a great cook. (*Pats his stomach*) I reckon this bears it out.

HELEN   (*To* LARRY)   I'd imagine real estate would take you outdoors a lot.

LARRY   It does.

HELEN   Then I'm surprised you don't have at least a slight tan.

ALBERT   (*To* HELEN)   You back to that again? (*To* LARRY) She gets a notion in her head she's like a dog with a bone. Say, why don't we go out on the town?

HELEN   I have a headache. I'm going to bed soon.

LARRY   And I'd prefer to stay right here.

ALBERT Party poops is what you both are. Say, it's getting warm in here. (*He goes to the window and opens it. The same trumpet sound is heard*) Don't he ever get tired blowing that thing? (*To* LARRY) We got a trumpet player lives upstairs. It's enough to drive you out of your mind.

HELEN He's a classical musician.

ALBERT He's classical all right. (*Slams the window shut*) I think the guy is a nance.

HELEN Why?

ALBERT You know why. (*To* LARRY) He's as old as us, not married, and lives with his mother. And you never saw a guy so pretty.

LARRY Except for the pretty part he sounds like me.

ALBERT Hell no, buddy. It's different in your case.

LARRY Why?

ALBERT Because I was there, Charlie. (*To* HELEN) Could I tell you stories about this man in the boo-dwar department.

HELEN (*To* LARRY) Next time you come bring your medals.

ALBERT (*To* LARRY) Ain't she got a sense of humor? Say, will you ever forget the night we liberated Paris? Man, I never saw such gratitude.

32

HELEN   Anybody got a cigar? (ALBERT *looks at her*) Well, isn't this a smoker?

ALBERT   I thought you were going to bed.

HELEN   My headache isn't bad enough yet. But it's getting there.

ALBERT   I was only trying to point up the difference between Larry's situation and that trumpet player's.

HELEN   He's on the road weeks at a time. How do you know what he does then? He might have hundreds of women. Probably does.

ALBERT   Why don't we just drop it?

HELEN   In favor of what? Oh I know: Let's talk about the farm. Larry was telling me you used to have your heart set on getting one. Now he says you can't remember ever feeling that way.

ALBERT   (*To* LARRY) That's the truth, buddy. The fact is I probably used to joke about it and you took me serious. . . . The same as I took you serious about being a doctor.

HELEN   That makes it a draw.

ALBERT   Say, did you ever bump into any of the old bunch?

LARRY   No.

33

ALBERT I did, once. Old Darrow. (*To* HELEN) You remember that bald guy we ran into at Grand Central about five years ago.

HELEN The one who kept scratching himself?

LARRY That sounds like Darrow.

ALBERT (*To* HELEN) Larry and I are going to be up all hours talking about old times and a lot of people you never heard of. Probably be boring for you, so any time you want to trot off to bed you do it. I mean don't just stay up to be polite on our account.

HELEN Isn't he considerate?

LARRY I always found him so.

HELEN Always gives his seat to old ladies in buses and I never saw him refuse a panhandler.

ALBERT What's wrong with that?

HELEN Who said anything was wrong? It's probably the answer to everything.

LARRY Where's the john?

ALBERT (*Points*) Through there.

LARRY Pardon me. (*Exits*)

34

ALBERT   God damn you. *God damn you.* . . . What must he be thinking?

HELEN   I'd like to know.

ALBERT   You're trying to drive him out of here. Well, you're not going to get away with it. When he comes back you're going to excuse yourself and go to bed.

HELEN   No.

ALBERT   Oh, yes you are. Believe me you are.

HELEN   He won't think you're so nice if you hit me.

ALBERT   I won't hit you but it'll be worse, so don't make me do it. . . . You know, he don't seem the way he was: cocky and wild and full of laughs. All he had to do was walk in a room and it lit up. I can't see any of that now. . . . Of course you sitting there casting a pall over everything don't help. But even taking that into account he's not at all the way I remember.

HELEN   Maybe you just don't remember right. Like you didn't remember right about the farm.

ALBERT   You *are* bound to make me explode.

HELEN   How could you forget those lovely rolling acres, that adorable antique of a house, the quaint lopsided barn, that heavenly mortgage?

ALBERT   A saint couldn't keep a good mood in this house. (LARRY *reënters*)Hey, you know what I was just thinking, buddy? It's a shame all the boys from the old outfit just drifted apart. I mean when you consider how close we all were and what we went through together, it don't seem right to lose track of each other that way.

LARRY   Can't be helped. People change. Their interests change. Finally they don't have anything in common except a memory that gets fainter every year.

ALBERT   That ain't true in every case. Take you and I. Hell, buddy, you saved my life. No amount of time is gonna change that. I'd do anything in the world for you and I know you'd do the same for me.

HELEN   Now you should cut wrists and drink each other's blood.

ALBERT   Isn't it time for you to go to bed, Helen?

HELEN   I'll go to bed when *I'm* ready to go.

ALBERT   All right ... all right. (*To* LARRY) Say, let me tell you about that kid of ours.

LARRY   I wish you would.

ALBERT   Well now, you should see him run. Fast as a deer. And climb ... Well, you'd think he was Tarzan. (*To* HELEN) Ain't he a great climber? (*To* LARRY) And say, funny. You

36

never heard a kid his age with such a fine sense of humor. (*To* HELEN) Keeps us in stitches, doesn't he? (*To* LARRY) And imagination—well, you never saw a kid with such a one as he has. (*To* HELEN) Will you ever forget the time he made out he was an elephant?

HELEN   I think I *will* go to bed.

ALBERT (*To* LARRY)   He went around on all fours for a week and we had to buy peanuts by the bushel basket.

HELEN   I'm going to bed.

ALBERT   What's that, dear?

HELEN   My headache is worse. I'm going to bed.

ALBERT   That's too bad. I was just going to suggest to Larry that we set up the trains so they'll be ready when young Larry comes home Christmas morning. (*To* LARRY) How about it?

LARRY   All right.

ALBERT (*To* HELEN)   You sure you don't want to watch us put up the kid's trains?
   (*She starts toward the bedroom*)

LARRY   It was nice meeting you. . . . I hope you feel better in the morning.
   (*At the door she stops and turns to* LARRY)

37

HELEN We don't call him Plowboy any more. Nobody does. Not for years.
> (*She exits into the bedroom and closes the door*)

ALBERT (*Moving to* LARRY *confidentially*) I guess you're wondering what that was all about? . . . Fact is she's due for her period. Always gets real skittish and peculiar just before that happens. Usually she's sweet as pie. . . . Say, I've got some pictures of the old bunch. Why don't I trot them out?

LARRY I thought we were going to set up the trains.

ALBERT Oh yeah.
> (LARRY *picks up the box containing the trains*)

LARRY I guess you'll want to run them around the tree.

ALBERT Yes.

LARRY Where will the tree be?

ALBERT We're getting one tomorrow.

LARRY Where will it be?

ALBERT (*Points*) There.
> (LARRY *goes to the designated place; opens the box*)

LARRY You tell young Larry any time he wants more track or any accessories he just has to go down to the store. The name's on the box. (*Holds up a car*) I think he'll get a real

kick out of this cattle car; the cows actually move into a
pen . . . (*He puts down that car; begins to extract others*)
You should see some of the gadgets they have.

ALBERT Say, buddy, I shouldn't let you go to all that trouble
now.

LARRY It's no trouble.

ALBERT No, buddy, I mean it. You leave those things be. I'll
put them up tomorrow.

LARRY I don't mind. I love trains. Besides, it's a tricky job.

ALBERT And you don't think the old Plowboy is smart enough
to figure it out on his own?

LARRY I didn't say that.

ALBERT I was just joking. But anyway you leave it all be and
relax yourself . . . I insist.

LARRY Okay.

ALBERT We've got a lot of talking to catch up on. For instance,
that Veronica. You and her were halfway down the aisle
near as I could figure. What happened, buddy?

LARRY Just one of those things.

ALBERT I remember when she came down to Camp Blanding.
You were almost going to get married right then and there.

39

And then all those letters you wrote one another while we were overseas. What went wrong?

LARRY   I told you: Just one of those things.

ALBERT   I figured if two people were ever going to stick, it was you and her. You fooled this country boy.

LARRY   You fooled easy in those days.

ALBERT   I guess so.

LARRY   How about now?

ALBERT   I've learned a few things.

LARRY   Such as?

ALBERT   Well, buddy, I don't keep my money in the mattress any more.

LARRY   Will you ever forget that?

ALBERT   I'm still sure it was Duffy who robbed me. No one else in the whole outfit chewed snuff and those were snuff stains on my pillow.

LARRY   You were ready to kill him.

ALBERT   I would have too, if you didn't talk me out of it.
        (*They both laugh. Then they look at each other a moment. Then both speak at once.*)

LARRY I'm surprised ...   ALBERT I never ...
(*They laugh*)

LARRY Go on.

ALBERT I was gonna say I never knew anyone with a better gift of gab than you had in those days. I was telling Helen before you got here that none of these jokers on the television make me laugh the way you used to.

LARRY As I recall, you laughed at everything.

ALBERT Say, I did, didn't I?

LARRY And it didn't matter how many times a thing was repeated.

ALBERT That's a fact. Like whenever someone would ask *you* where somebody was. You'd say, "He's lying down over in the corner, drunker than hell, but better than he was." I always got a bang out of that.

LARRY Doesn't seem funny now, does it?

ALBERT It was the way you used to come out with it. (*Silence*) What were you surprised about?

LARRY What?

ALBERT You started to say you were surprised before. About what?

LARRY About you being content to live in the city.

ALBERT Who said I was content?

LARRY Well then, what are you doing here?

ALBERT Damn, but it's warm in here. (*Opens the window*) Well what do you know: Our trumpet player stopped . . . Either we get too much heat like tonight or they don't send up nearly enough. I guess that's one nice thing about Florida, huh? Yes sir, I could take to those sunny beaches with no strain at all.

LARRY If you don't like the city, why stay?

ALBERT Who said I don't like the city?

LARRY You said you weren't content here.

ALBERT That ain't necessarily the city's fault.

LARRY Whose fault is it?

ALBERT Buddy, I expected to have some laughs tonight. I figured by this time we'd both be drunk as skunks. Come on, loosen up. Have a beer.

LARRY No.

ALBERT You know something? You have a funny look in your eye. You haven't gone religious, have you?

LARRY No.

ALBERT Well, praise the Lord.
     (*Drinks*)

LARRY You've got a job, a family, a home. You're in good
health. Why aren't you content? What's wrong?

ALBERT Who said anything was wrong?

LARRY *You* did.

ALBERT Say, why *don't* we set up those trains. I'm bound to
botch it up if I do it myself. . . . Say, they're real cute, aren't
they?

LARRY What about the farm?

ALBERT Hey, how about this caboose?

LARRY Plowboy?

ALBERT And that pullman—you can actually see the people.

LARRY *Plowboy!*

ALBERT What?

LARRY Why didn't you go back to the farm?

ALBERT (*Pauses*) I did. . . . Bought a place in Pennsylvania . . .
House . . . barn . . . chickens . . . cows. The works. . . . Took

43

every cent I could beg or borrow. . . . All down the drain inside of two years.

LARRY What went wrong?

ALBERT Me. . . . We got there at night. The people I bought it from turned over the keys and left. We went to bed but I couldn't sleep. I thought it was the excitement of having my dream come true, but as the night went on I realized there was nothing good in my feeling. . . . Four-thirty the alarm went off. Helen made breakfast. I couldn't eat a thing. . . . I stepped out of the house. The sky was beginning to get light. I stood in the doorway. I could see fields of corn and lettuce and beans and tomatoes. . . . I could hear pigs and chickens and cows and horses. And everything that I could hear belonged to me. . . . And right then, right at that instant, it hit me what was wrong. . . . I didn't know anything about farming.

LARRY What do you mean?

ALBERT I mean all that I could see and hear was my responsibility to care for and I didn't know the first god damn thing to do.

LARRY But you lived on a farm till you were twelve.

ALBERT Yes, but I didn't remember anything. And no wonder when I really thought about it. My father did everything. My mother wouldn't let me help. She hated the farm. She was determined I was not to follow in his footsteps. So all I used to do was loll around playing. And standing there

44

that morning I remembered all that for the first time. . . . Buddy, I was paralyzed. . . . The sky was getting brighter so I could see all my responsibilities clearer. And the animals kept making more and more noise to be cared for. You never heard such a racket. And I just stood there watching and listening till Helen came and shook the truth out of me. . . . After she got through cursing me she sent me to town to get a hired man. Even with the hired man I didn't manage. I didn't have any talent for it. More important, I didn't have any love for it. To be honest, I hated it. I was my mother's boy in spades.

LARRY   Why didn't you tell me this before?

ALBERT   I was ashamed. I'd sold you a phony bill of goods. Hell, it was you that named me Plowboy. What must you be thinking now?

LARRY   I'm thinking that maybe it was my fault. Maybe *I* was the one who sold *you* the bill of goods.

ALBERT   Don't talk nonsense. I looked like a plowboy, talked like a plowboy, and thought I was one long before I ever met you.

LARRY   But did you think of getting a farm before you met me?

ALBERT   Yes.

LARRY   That would explain why your wife looked at me the way she did. She feels I'm responsible for the farm.

45

ALBERT   I tell you it was my idea.

LARRY   Back to your roots. The virtues and joy of a rustic existence! I remember the lectures I used to give. My God, *was* I responsible?

ALBERT   No. Now drop it.

LARRY   You want to know something? . . . I'm relieved. . . . I got the feeling from your wife that I was being indicted for the worst crime on earth. I'm relieved to know that this is all she accuses me of.

ALBERT   She don't accuse you of anything.

LARRY   Then why is she so angry?

ALBERT   She's not angry. I told you before she's due for the curse. It affects some women that way. Now damn it to hell you need a beer and I'm going to see you have one if I have to pour it down your throat.
        (*He would put his beer glass to* LARRY's *lips but* LARRY *shoves his hand away angrily*)

LARRY   *I didn't come here to drink beer!*

ALBERT   *What did you come for?* (*Silence*) Let's get busy with these trains. (*He starts assembling the tracks*) I guess it don't matter which tracks connect with which.

LARRY   I came to see if you were happy.

46

ALBERT Now what's *this* wire for?

LARRY *Are* you happy?

ALBERT Is that all you came here for; just to ask me that?

LARRY Yes.

ALBERT Well, now I'm the one who's relieved. Helen figured that you were really after something. That you wanted something like money or something. You've been acting so strange that I was beginning to think maybe she was right. Of course, I'd give you anything if you asked me for it. But the fact is I don't have hardly anything *to* give so I'm relieved to know that that's all you want. Now come on and help me with the trains. I can't figure this wire sticking out of this one track here.

LARRY You haven't answered the question. . . . *Are* you happy?
    (*Silence*)

ALBERT No.

LARRY Not at all?
    (ALBERT *shakes his head no*)

ALBERT You know the only things that make me get up in the morning? . . . Booze and the chance of running into a piece while I'm on my route. It doesn't happen very often, the piece I mean, but now and then you come across a live one. It happened yesterday. I was reading meters in Brook-

47

lyn in this dame's apartment and out of a clear blue sky she begins to ask me what I think of husbands who play around. It seems her husband was that sort and she had just learned about it. Well, I said to her, in my opinion she should fight fire with fire. It turned out to be a most pleasant morning. Now—

LARRY   I get the picture.

ALBERT   Let me finish, buddy. There's a great punch line. . . . You see, when I got dressed I put her husband's socks on by mistake. Helen was darning them when you came in. How's that for a close one?

LARRY   Charming.

ALBERT   You don't approve?

LARRY   What's there to approve?

ALBERT   Well, I thought a big ass man like you would surely approve. . . . What's the matter, buddy, you look a little ill. I'm sorry if I disgusted you but you insisted on sticking your nose in and asking questions so I want to be sure and give you the answers in full. Like for instance about that job driving a truck.

LARRY   I think you better go to bed.

ALBERT   I told you I gave it up because there was no future in it. What I meant was there was no future in it for me. You see, there's always some kind of hassle going when you drive

48

a truck and I couldn't take it. After two weeks I was shaking like a leaf. One day in the middle of a traffic jam on Thirty-fourth Street I got out of my truck, walked away and left it there. It was in all the papers, buddy. How'd you miss it? (LARRY *rises*) What do you want? Do you want something?

LARRY I'm leaving.

ALBERT (*Blocks his way*) No you ain't. You came here to find out if I was happy and you're not going out of here without a complete answer. You try to go and I'll knock you down. *God damn it, somebody has to listen to me!*

LARRY All right ... go on.

ALBERT That's my buddy. But, buddy, where were you ten years ago? I needed you then. I needed to talk to somebody and you were the only one and I couldn't find you. I tried everything. Well, you're here now. Maybe it's not too late. Helen says it's too late but maybe she's wrong. She's like her mother. Gloomy . . . gloomy. Gloomy. Gloomy. You know what I call her mother? . . . Old moaning low. Old everything happens for the worst. . . . You know the only thing they look forward to? . . . Dying. . . . That's right: Dying. . . . One time Helen and I had a terrible fight. I started to choke her. Had my hands around her neck and meant to kill her. You know what stopped me? . . . She never struggled. I was doing just what she wanted. . . . She never forgave me for stopping.

LARRY I can't hear any more. I'm sorry but I can't.
     (*He starts to put on his overcoat*)

49

ALBERT You've got to! You owe it to me. (LARRY *regards him incredulously*) That's right, *you* owe it to me. If it wasn't for you I wouldn't be here, *so you owe it to me!*
    (*In desperation he seizes the lapels of* LARRY's *coat*)

LARRY You son of a bitch! (*Hurls him to the floor*) You lousy son of a bitch!

ALBERT Take me to Florida. Give me a job. Talk to me. Help me, buddy. Save the Plowboy again. (LARRY *exits and slams the door, which rouses* ALBERT, *who runs after him out into the hallway*) You haven't heard the worst part. If you heard that you'd understand. You would, buddy. (*Calls down the stairwell*) Don't go, buddy. Don't go. (*There is a crashing noise from downstairs*) Buddy! . . . *Buddy!* (ALBERT *runs down the stairs.* HELEN, *attracted by the commotion, comes into the living room. Now* ALBERT *appears carrying* LARRY, *who is unconscious. He brings him into the apartment. To* HELEN) He collapsed. He started downstairs and just crumpled up. . . . Call the doctor. (*She goes to the phone and dials while he lays* LARRY *on the couch; clucks at him*) Buddy . . . buddy, wake up . . . buddy . . . buddy . . .

Curtain

Scene Two

It is about an hour later.

At rise, HELEN *and* ALBERT *sit on opposite sides of the room. An overcoat is draped over a chair. There is a hat beside it.* ALBERT *keeps darting nervous glances toward the off-stage bedroom.*

ALBERT   What's his name again?

HELEN   Sheldon.

ALBERT   I don't see why Dr. Block couldn't come.

HELEN   I told you: Block doesn't feel well himself.

ALBERT   He's certainly taking his time. . . . I'd feel better if it was Block in there . . . (*Rises, paces aimlessly, stops at the coat, examines the lapel*) Expensive taste. I can see what he's gonna charge. (*Eyes the off-stage bedroom again*) He's been in there half an hour. How much longer is he gonna take? . . . Did you hear Larry then?

HELEN   No.

ALBERT I figure it was just the excitement of coming to New York and all. . . . I hope he snaps out of it before his mother gets here.

HELEN What did you tell her?

ALBERT That he wasn't feeling well and I thought it would be better if he spent the night here.

HELEN Was she excited?

ALBERT No, but she insisted on coming up. I'm sorry as hell now I called. . . . What the devil is taking that doctor so long. . . . This started out to be a wonderful night. How did it end up like this? (*Picks up the doctor's hat and looks inside it*) This is no ten-dollar hat either. Don't pay this guy cash. That's how these jokers beat their income tax. Make him send a bill.
       (*The bedroom door opens and the* DOCTOR *comes out, closing the door behind him*)

DOCTOR He appears to be suffering from complete exhaustion.

ALBERT (*To* HELEN) What did I tell you?

DOCTOR I gave him a sedative that should allow him to sleep well into the morning. Of course I can only make a superficial diagnosis under these conditions.

ALBERT Oh, it's exhaustion all right. I could see how tired he was the minute he got here. Usually he's very lively, so I knew something was wrong right away.

DOCTOR Yes. Well, you bring him to my office tomorrow. Here's my card. The hours are twelve to two.
(*Starts to put on his hat and coat*)

ALBERT How much do I owe you?

DOCTOR I'll send you a bill. Goodnight.

ALBERT Goodnight.

HELEN Goodnight, Doctor.
(*He exits*)

ALBERT What did I tell you? Didn't I say it was just exhaustion? I'm sorry as hell now that I called his mother.

HELEN How do you suppose he got so exhausted?

ALBERT Probably been on a bender. Probably never gave up booze at all. You wait and see: a good night's sleep and you won't even recognize him. He'll be his old self. . . . Probably won't remember anything that happened tonight.

HELEN You hope. (*He turns to her*) Sounded like a nice little row you were having. What was it about?

ALBERT Nothing.

HELEN Did you find out what he wanted?

53

ALBERT   He doesn't want anything.

HELEN   Did he offer you a job?

ALBERT   We didn't talk about that.

HELEN   You didn't get very far putting up the trains, did you?
(*The doorbell rings*)

ALBERT   That's the upstairs bell. Probably his mother.

HELEN   Well, let her in.

ALBERT   We mustn't excite her. She's an old lady.

HELEN   Open the door.
(*He goes to the door*)

ALBERT   Come in, Mrs. Doyle. Come in. (MRS. DOYLE, *a woman in her late sixties, enters.* ALBERT *closes the door*) That's some climb coming up those stairs. Here, give me your coat. (*Helps her off with her coat*) Larry's sleeping like a lamb. Doctor just left. Said it was a plain and simple case of exhaustion. I'm sorry I put you to all this trouble for nothing.

MRS. DOYLE   How much did the doctor charge?

ALBERT   He's going to send a bill.

54

MRS. DOYLE (*Takes a bill from her purse and offers it to him*) Five dollars should be enough. Here.

ALBERT   That isn't necessary.

MRS. DOYLE   I insist.

ALBERT (*Sees how adamant she is and takes the bill*)   All right, but it isn't necessary. I'd be only too glad—

MRS. DOYLE   I'm sure you would. . . . Where is he?

ALBERT   In the bedroom. (*Ushers her into the living room*) This is my wife Helen.

HELEN   Hello.

MRS. DOYLE   How do you do.
          (*The two women regard each other*)

ALBERT   It's a shame we all had to meet under these circumstances. . . . Say, how would you like a nice cup of tea?

MRS. DOYLE   Thank you, not just now.

ALBERT   Well, you sing out if you change your mind. I know from Larry what a great one you are for your tea. (*She sits.* ALBERT *indicates the off-stage bedroom*) He's in that room there, if you want to take a look at him.

MRS. DOYLE   Not just now, thank you.
          (*Unaware of how uneasy she is making them, she looks*

55

about, from where she is seated, blatantly inspecting the apartment)

ALBERT   The doctor says he'll sleep well into the morning. . . .
(*She continues looking about*) We don't put our Christmas
decorations up till Christmas Eve. . . . (*As her eye falls on
the trains*) It was swell of Larry to bring those trains. . . .
Young Larry will be here Christmas morning. He's upstate
visiting some relatives. . . . I guess Larry got a real kick out
of me naming the kid after him.

MRS. DOYLE   He did.

ALBERT   I figured it was the least I could do for him.
(*She continues looking around*)

HELEN   If you're looking for the bathroom, it's through there.
(*To* ALBERT) Mrs. Doyle seems to be looking for something.
I thought maybe it was the bathroom.

MRS. DOYLE   No, but thank you anyway.

ALBERT (*To* HELEN)   Mrs. Doyle used to send us packages of
things she'd canned herself. Greatest stuff I ever tasted. (*To*
MRS. DOYLE) Do you still can?

MRS. DOYLE   No.

ALBERT   We're having a very mild winter but I guess it still
seems pretty bad to you.

56

MRS. DOYLE   Why?

ALBERT   Well, I mean in contrast to Florida.

MRS. DOYLE   I come from Chicago.

ALBERT   I thought you lived in Florida with Larry.

MRS. DOYLE   I'll see him now. (*She rises.* ALBERT *rises with her*) I can manage alone.
   (*She goes off into the bedroom*)

ALBERT   What gave me the idea she lived with Larry?

HELEN   He did. He said he was like the trumpet player because he lived with his mother.

ALBERT   We must have misunderstood him.

HELEN   Listen to me.

ALBERT   What?

HELEN   Get her out of here. I don't care what excuse you use but get rid of her as fast as you can.

ALBERT   Why?

HELEN   She gives me the creeps.

ALBERT   She's upset about Larry.

HELEN   So upset she sat here and looked over the whole room before she went in to see him. What the devil was she looking for?. . . And we didn't misunderstand him. He *did* say he lived with her.

ALBERT   Don't be ridiculous. Why would he lie about a thing like that?

HELEN   I don't know. I just want her out of my house. I want them both out.

ALBERT   Larry can't be moved.

HELEN   Well, get rid of *her*. I—(MRS. DOYLE *reappears*) How is he?

MRS. DOYLE   Asleep.

ALBERT   He gave us quite a scare.

MRS. DOYLE   Did he?

HELEN   We'd offer to put you up for the night but we don't have the room.

MRS. DOYLE   Thank you, I'll return to the hotel.

ALBERT   You must be pretty tired.

58

MRS. DOYLE   Yes.

HELEN   In that case we mustn't keep you any longer. (*To* AL-
BERT) Get Mrs. Doyle's coat.

ALBERT   I think she should have a cup of tea before she goes.

HELEN   We're out of tea.

ALBERT   Are you sure?

HELEN   Yes.

ALBERT   (*To* MRS. DOYLE)   I'm sorry.

HELEN   Get the coat.

ALBERT   All right.
        (*He gets* MRS. DOYLE's *coat and holds it for her. She
        dons it absently*)

MRS. DOYLE   What else did Larry tell you?

ALBERT   About what?

MRS. DOYLE   About himself.

ALBERT   Just that he lived in Florida and was doing very
nicely in the real estate business.

MRS. DOYLE   It's not true.

59

ALBERT What's not true?

MRS. DOYLE None of it. . . . Not about Florida or the real estate or any of it. . . . All lies.

HELEN (*To* ALBERT) Go down and get Mrs. Doyle a cab. When you have one, tick the button for her to come.

ALBERT All right.
(*Turns and starts toward the door*)

MRS. DOYLE Don't you want to know why he lied?

ALBERT (*Stops*) No . . . No, I don't think I do.

HELEN Then go for the cab.

ALBERT Yes.
(*He continues toward the door*)

MRS. DOYLE He's dying.
(ALBERT *falters as though he might stop*)

HELEN *Go for the cab!*
(*He continues toward the door*)

MRS. DOYLE It's your fault.
(*This stops him. He turns to her*)

HELEN You fool.
(*She turns away from both of them*)

MRS. DOYLE Dying and it's your fault.

ALBERT My fault?

MRS. DOYLE The wound . . . the wound he got when he saved you.

ALBERT He recovered from that.

MRS. DOYLE So he thought. And so it seemed for several years. Then it began to bother him. He's been in one hospital or another ever since. Now they say in a matter of months he'll be dead and he knows it. . . . He didn't want you to find out. He didn't want you to blame yourself.

HELEN Then why did he come here?

MRS. DOYLE He never said, but I think it was to convince himself that he had not sacrificed his life for nothing.

ALBERT Oh, my God.

MRS. DOYLE If you are happy, then he accomplished something.

ALBERT My God.

MRS. DOYLE He must not know that I've told you any of this.

HELEN Why *have* you told us?

MRS. DOYLE Because my intuition tells me this is by no means a happy home. If my son hasn't discovered that, I beg you—prevent his doing so. (*Looks toward* ALBERT) Did you know *he* was married? A good match, and on his way to being a fine doctor. Number one in his class. All the best in front of him when that old sore began to act up. When he realized there would be nothing but hospitals for the rest of his life he made an end of the marriage. Did it in fine style, as usual, so she wouldn't blame herself. . . . I always live a block from the hospital. . . . Too graceful—that was his trouble. Anyone could lean against him and as hard as they wanted. And never a peep out of him.

ALBERT You must hate me.

MRS. DOYLE Yes. . . . I'll go now. I can get my own cab. (*Starts for the door, then halts*) No child lives in this house.

HELEN No.

MRS. DOYLE Does he know that?

HELEN No.

MRS. DOYLE Good.
      (*She exits.* HELEN *and* ALBERT *stand silently for a time*)

ALBERT I'll take tomorrow off. . . . You get prettied up soon as you get out of bed. . . . We'll be all smiles. All lovey-dovey. . . . First thing in the morning I'll get Christmas decorations and a Christmas tree and presents. . . . I'll

smooth everything over. . . . Time I get through he'll think
this is the happiest place he ever saw. . . . I'll get a big tree.
Not one of them midgets. . . . I'll tell him the kid insisted
on a big tree . . .

(*As he talks the Curtain slowly descends*)

ACT TWO

ACT TWO

It is the following morning.

At rise, HELEN *stands by the open window listening to the trumpet. She appears nervous. The trains which Larry brought have been set up. The doorbell rings—three times long, two times short.* HELEN *closes the window, and opens the door to admit* ALBERT, *who carries a Christmas tree, a stand and several boxes of lights and ornaments.*

HELEN   What took you so long?

ALBERT   I had to go all the way to Broadway to get a tree. Five bucks for this. Can you beat it? ... He still sleeping?

HELEN   Yes. I thought you'd never get back.

ALBERT   I was only gone a half-hour.

HELEN   I was afraid he'd wake up while you were out.

ALBERT   What if he did?

HELEN   I don't want to be alone with him.

ALBERT   Why not?

HELEN I'm afraid I'll say the wrong thing, that I won't act right.

ALBERT You don't give yourself enough credit. (*Holds the tree up*) Here, give me a hand. (*She moves to assist him*) This is supposed to be the latest thing in stands. You hold the tree like that and I'll screw these things into it.

HELEN (*As they put up the tree*) How much did you tell him last night?

ALBERT Don't worry about that. . . . Will you hold the tree straight.

HELEN You were arguing.

ALBERT I can smooth that over. Stop jiggling the tree. . . . And about us—I mean you and me. Well, if we seemed in a bad mood last night, it was because we had a little spat before he got here.

HELEN About what?

ALBERT You wanted a new coat and I said no. It was one of those little spats that got out of hand. To spite you I started drinking too much. When I drink too much I get very depressed. I exaggerate my troubles. . . . I'm not getting anywhere with this thing.

68

HELEN Let me do it.

ALBERT No! You're always complaining how clumsy I am. Well, what the devil do you expect when you never give me a chance to finish anything. . . . Will you please hold the damn thing straight. . . . I told him about the farm . . . the whole story.

HELEN How you going to smooth *that* over?

ALBERT I'm not going to try. Everyone has to have some disappointments. . . . Remember: His mother wasn't here. I never called her. I wanted to but I couldn't remember the name of the hotel.

HELEN He'll wonder what the doctor said.

ALBERT We'll tell him: exhaustion. (*Catches his finger in the stand*) Ow! . . . Damn it to hell, I caught my finger.

HELEN Here.
    (*He now supports the tree, while she sets up the stand*)

ALBERT (*Sucking the injured finger*) Gave myself a nice cut.

HELEN Are you sure you've told me everything you said last night, so we don't contradict each other.

69

ALBERT   Uh huh. . . . This thing's really bleeding.

HELEN   Don't move the tree.

ALBERT   You know something: You look very nice this morning . . . I like the way your hair is. (*No reply*) I said I like the way your hair is.

HELEN   Save it. (*She secures the tree and rises*) There.
         (*He seizes her arm*)

ALBERT   I hope to God you're going to cooperate. I hope you ain't going to spoil this thing.

HELEN   I'll do my best.
         (*She frees herself and begins to decorate the tree*)

ALBERT   If you say the wrong thing it won't be any accident and I'll know it. (*Listens*) He's moving around . . . he's getting up. Now don't be nervous. . . . Come here.

HELEN   What do you want?

ALBERT   *Come here!*
         (*She comes to him apprehensively*)

HELEN   What do you want?

ALBERT   Put your arms around me.

HELEN   I will not.
(*He grabs her and forces her to him so they are in something of an embrace when* LARRY, *wearing pajamas and a robe, both much too big for him, appears*)

LARRY   Good morning.
(ALBERT *and* HELEN *separate with something that could pass for embarrassment*)

ALBERT   Good morning, and excuse us.

LARRY   I should have knocked. (*To* HELEN) Good morning.

HELEN   Good morning.

ALBERT   How you feel, buddy?

LARRY   Fine. I don't know what happened to me last night.

ALBERT   Doctor said it was just a plain and simple case of exhaustion.

LARRY   That figures. I've been going at quite a pace.

ALBERT   Well, maybe I'm speaking out of turn, but I've got to tell you for your own good that you can't keep chasing around like you did when we were youngsters. No sir. The time comes when you have to single out one filly, grab her . . .
(*He grabs* HELEN *around the waist and swings her in a circle*)

HELEN Stop it!

ALBERT Eh-yah! (*Deposits her*) And settle down. That's what you've got to do, buddy: Settle down.

LARRY Maybe you're right.

ALBERT I know I am.

LARRY What time is it?

HELEN Ten thirty.

LARRY (*To* ALBERT) What time do you go to work?

ALBERT I'm not going today. Phoned in sick.

LARRY You didn't have to do that on my account.

ALBERT Don't talk nonsense. Say, hadn't you better call your mother and let her know where you are?

LARRY Yes.

ALBERT I was going to do it but I couldn't remember which hotel you said it was.

LARRY The Statler. Where's the phone?

72

ALBERT   In the foyer there.

LARRY   I better do that right now.
(*He goes into the foyer and phones. We can't hear the call*)

HELEN   I'll go along with all this. I'll—

ALBERT   I hope his mother doesn't give it away.

HELEN   Listen to me.

ALBERT   What?

HELEN   I'll go along with all this. I'll smile and laugh and do everything I can to make him think we get along fine, but don't put your hands on me.

ALBERT   I was just—

HELEN   You were just taking advantage of the situation.

ALBERT   I was not. I was only trying to be convincing.

HELEN   A lot of couples get along fine and they don't paw each other in public.

ALBERT   A lot of couples, maybe. Not us. When *we* got along best we were at each other every minute. In public or not.

73

HELEN   Don't be disgusting.
   (LARRY *completes his call; returns to them*)

ALBERT   You get her?

LARRY   Yes.

ALBERT   (*Hanging ornaments on the tree*)   Everything all right?

LARRY   Everything's fine.

ALBERT   She wasn't too worried, I hope.

LARRY   No. She's used to my irregular hours.

ALBERT   That's good.

HELEN (*To* LARRY)   Will you have some breakfast?

ALBERT   Of course he will.

LARRY (*To* HELEN)   Well, I would like some coffee, thank you.

ALBERT   Just coffee? What the devil kind of a breakfast do you call that? We've got eggs, bacon, cereal, anything you want. Just name it.

74

LARRY All I want is coffee.

ALBERT Well, I certainly—

HELEN Larry's old enough to know what he wants for breakfast.

LARRY Thank you.

HELEN Cream and sugar?

LARRY Just cream.
   (*She exits to the kitchen*)

ALBERT Is that all you have every morning? Coffee?

LARRY Usually. Why?

ALBERT Well then, it's no damn wonder you . . .

LARRY It's no wonder I what?

ALBERT Well, that you look so scrawny and go around col-
lapsing from exhaustion. Man, breakfast is the most important meal of the day. It's like the foundation of a house.

LARRY I'll make a note of it. (ALBERT *looks at him a moment
and laughs*) What's funny?

75

ALBERT You should see yourself in my pajamas. You look like one of them floppy clowns.

LARRY I do feel kind of lonely in here.

ALBERT Hey, do you remember that crazy boy from Baltimore who took his pajamas into combat?

LARRY Novak?

ALBERT Yeah. Swore he was gonna wear them every night as some kind of protest against the war.

LARRY And then loused up the whole idea by getting killed the first day we saw action.

ALBERT Say, that's right, he *was* killed, wasn't he?

LARRY Uh huh.

ALBERT Well, now isn't that a cheerful thing to be discussing first thing in the morning. I wonder what the devil made me bring up a thing like that.

LARRY We were talking about pajamas.

ALBERT That's right. That's what it was.

LARRY I see you bought a tree.

76

ALBERT   Yeah. Kind of skimpy-looking but it was the best they had left. Young Larry's gonna be mad. He likes a big one.

(LARRY *opens one of the boxes* ALBERT *brought in*)

LARRY   New lights?

ALBERT   Our old ones were shot, and it don't pay to take chances when there's a kid around. You're always reading something about kids getting burned at this time of year.

LARRY   (*Regarding the decorations on the tree*)   I always thought you put the lights on first.

ALBERT   You're right. . . . How do you like that? . . . Say, listen, while Helen's out of the room I want to tell you that I hope you didn't get me wrong about what I said before about settling down. I mean I hope I didn't sound like I was trying to give you the idea that marriage is nothing but paradise. I didn't, did I?

LARRY   No.

ALBERT   That's good. Married guys are always sounding off like that to bachelors. You know, "Come on in, the water's fine." And it don't matter a damn if the water is ten below zero. You and I are too close for crap like that. I mean I'll level with you about marriage. The plain fact is that it ain't all beer and skittles, by a long shot. No sir. But still, over the long pull, it's the only way to really live.

77

LARRY   This off the record or can I quote you?

ALBERT   I'm serious, buddy. Now of course appearances are de-
ceiving. Take Helen and me: Most people meet us they
think we never exchanged a cross word in our lives. Of
course that would be hard for you to believe. From what you
heard last night you probably got the notion we battle all the
time. Well, the actual truth is somewhere between those
two points. That is to say that while we're not always lovey-
dovey, still we're nothing like the impression we must have
given you last night.

LARRY   You don't have to explain about last night.

ALBERT   I do. I certainly do. I won't have you leaving here
with any wrong ideas about us. Now what happened last
night was that Helen and me had a row before you got
here. One of those little stupid things that got blown up
way out of reason. She wants a certain coat. I thought it was
too expensive. I said no. She said something back about the
money I spend on beer. And bingo, we're off. It ends up
with me drinking too much to spite her. Then you called
and said you were coming. Well, by that time I was already
tight. You know how some guys get depressed when they
get tight?

LARRY   Yeah.

ALBERT   Well, that's how it hits me. I always feel way down
and sorry for myself. Any little problems I have take on the
size of mountains. I don't remember everything I said to

you but I know a lot of it was pretty wild and I apologize.

LARRY Forget it.

ALBERT The fact is Helen and I are as happy as any couple we know. . . . We'll be married twelve years in April.

LARRY Maybe the thing for you to do is to give up booze.

ALBERT You know something—I think you're right. Seems I always end up the morning after apologizing for a lot of bull I said the night before.

LARRY About the farm. Was that bull?

ALBERT No. No, that was true. But still it wasn't the tragedy like I made out. It was just one of those disappointments that happens to everyone. I got over it. It never even crosses my mind except when I'm drinking.
    (HELEN *enters with coffee and toast, which she sets before* LARRY)

HELEN There's some toast and jelly there in case you change your mind.

LARRY Thank you.

ALBERT (*To* LARRY, *indicating* HELEN) If you lived around here she'd have you fattened up in no time.

LARRY   I'll bet.

ALBERT   (*To* HELEN, *indicating* LARRY)   Would you ever believe that such a runt as that was able to lug me on his back for fifty yards? (*The phone rings*) I'll get it.
(*Goes to the phone.* LARRY *and* HELEN *regard each other. She is now the uneasy one*)

HELEN   The coffee's very hot.
(LARRY *tries the coffee and puts it down*)

LARRY   Thanks for the warning.

HELEN   Burn yourself?

LARRY   Not quite.
(*Pause*)

HELEN   We like our coffee hot. . . . I hope it isn't too strong. We like it that way.

LARRY   The stronger the better.

HELEN   That's how we feel. Anything we can't stand is a weak cup of coffee. . . . Without snow it doesn't seem like Christmas, does it?

LARRY   No.

HELEN   I hope you found the bed comfortable.

LARRY   I did. (*Tries the coffee again*) Still too hot. I think I'll get dressed while it's cooling. Will you pardon me?

HELEN   Certainly.
(*He goes into the bedroom.* ALBERT *hangs up*)

HELEN   Who was that?

ALBERT   Gavigan.

HELEN   What did he want?

ALBERT   I have to go to the office.

HELEN   I thought you told him you were sick.

ALBERT   The supervisor came around and a couple of my sheets aren't in order. It'll only take an hour.

HELEN   Don't go.

ALBERT   I have to. What's he doing?

HELEN   Getting dressed. . . . Wait till he has his coffee, then take him with you.

ALBERT   No.

HELEN   Why not?

ALBERT I told him the story I made up to cover last night, but I don't think he believed me.

HELEN Is he apt to believe you any better if he hangs around here?

ALBERT I won't let him go away thinking about us the way he does now.

HELEN If he stays he might end up thinking a lot worse.

ALBERT You just keep him here till I get back. I'll fix everything.

HELEN How? What can you do?

ALBERT Just keep him here. I'll think of something. I have to. I can't let him go like this. (*Goes to the bedroom door*) Hey, buddy?

LARRY (*From off stage*) Yeah?

ALBERT I got to run down to my office for a few minutes. I'll see you when I get back.

LARRY (*From off stage*) I was going to shove off pretty soon.

HELEN (*To* ALBERT) Let him go. Please.

ALBERT (*Ignores her*) You can stay a little longer.
(LARRY *comes out buttoning his shirt*)

LARRY   I promised my mother I'd take her to Radio City.

ALBERT   You'll have time. I'll just be a few minutes. Okay? . . .
Okay?

LARRY   Okay.

ALBERT   That a boy. (*Puts on his coat*) Be back in three
shakes. Bye, hon. (*Kisses* HELEN, *who can't help averting
her head*) Married twelve years and still blushes. How about
that?

HELEN   Albert, really.

ALBERT   See ya.
      (*Exits*)

LARRY   Same old Plowboy.

HELEN   Yes.

LARRY   I forgot they don't call him that any more.
      (*He takes some of his coffee*)

HELEN   Is there enough cream in it?

LARRY   Yes. . . . When did they stop calling him Plowboy?

HELEN   Years ago. (*He drinks the coffee.*) It's probably cold
now. I'll warm it up.

LARRY   It's perfectly all right the way it is. . . . Why did they stop?

HELEN   Pardon me?

LARRY   Why did everyone stop calling him Plowboy?

HELEN   They just did. . . . If you'll excuse me I think I'll clean up my kitchen.

LARRY   You really can't stand me, can you?

HELEN   Why do you say that?

LARRY   You won't even sit and talk awhile.

HELEN   If you want me to sit and talk I'll be glad to.

LARRY   Look, I know why you don't like me and I don't blame you. In a way I guess I was responsible.

HELEN   For what?

LARRY   The farm. Albert told me about it last night.

HELEN   Oh.

LARRY   I did name him Plowboy. And I did fill his head with a lot of talk about quitting the city and going back to the

country where he belonged. So I guess I am partly responsible for what he did, and you have every right to blame me
for it.

HELEN   I don't blame *you* for that.

LARRY   Then what is it?

HELEN   What is what?

LARRY   Why are you so nervous? Why do you look at me the
way you do?

HELEN   What way?

LARRY   Like I was your worst enemy.

HELEN   What are you talking about?

LARRY   I'm talking about the hate in your eyes when you look
at me.

HELEN   I never met you before last night. What reason could
I have to feel one way or another about you?

LARRY   It's in your eyes right now!

HELEN   I think I better clean up the kitchen.
       (*Turns from him and starts toward the kitchen*)

LARRY (*Blocking her way*) *If it's the money, tell me how much the farm set you back and I'll make it good!*
(*She looks at him as though he'd struck her, then about to cry, runs to the kitchen*)

LARRY (*Calls*) Excuse the last remark. It was uncalled for. . . . As a matter of fact forget everything I said . . . (*Drinks the coffee*) The coffee is excellent. . . . A man should never open his mouth in the morning until he's had his coffee . . . (*Goes to the kitchen door and listens*) Please don't cry. . . . There's nothing to cry about. . . . *Will you please stop crying . . .* (*Unable to stand the sound of her crying he goes to the piano, opens it, and, reading a piece of music already on the holder, begins to play loudly in an effort to drown her out*) Let me know when you're through.
(HELEN *appears immediately in the kitchen doorway*)

HELEN Don't do that . . . don't play.

LARRY (*Goes on playing*) Am I that bad?

HELEN Please stop.

LARRY (*As he plays*) I'll make a deal. You stop crying and I'll stop playing.

HELEN You must stop.

LARRY Well, how about it? Is it a deal?

86

HELEN I said stop!
(She goes to the piano and pulls the sheet music from the stand. He stops and now aware for the first time of her intensity regards her curiously)

HELEN I'm sorry ... I don't like anyone to touch my piano ... I asked you to stop ... I can't stand for anyone to touch my piano.

LARRY Why?

HELEN I just can't. I realize how childish that sounds, but I can't.
(Someone rattles the doorknob. HELEN seems not to hear the sound)

LARRY There's someone at the door.

HELEN I've always been like that about my possessions.
(The rattling of the door handle is repeated)

LARRY Someone's at your door.

HELEN It's the kids. They're always doing that. If you don't pay any attention they go away.
(Now there is a gentle tapping at the door)

LARRY I'll get rid of them.
(He starts for the door)

HELEN   No. I'll go. . . . I know them. (*She moves toward the door. Then pauses. The knock is repeated*) It's probably the kids.

> (*Again the knock sounds. She goes to the door with great reluctance, would open it only partially but the man who was knocking enters boldly*)

THE MAN   Why was it locked? (HELEN *just looks at him*) What's wrong? (*Now he follows her gaze and turns to face* LARRY) Who are you?

LARRY   Friend of the family.

THE MAN   (*To* HELEN)   What's going on here?

LARRY   You took the words right out of my mouth.

HELEN   (*To* THE MAN, *indicating* LARRY)   He's a friend of Albert's.

THE MAN   (*To* LARRY)   So am I, I live upstairs. (*To* HELEN) Mother wanted to know if she could borrow a cup of sugar.

LARRY   Where's the cup?

HELEN   (*To* THE MAN)   We can spare him the performance.

LARRY   Thank you.

THE MAN   I think I better go. (*To* LARRY) If you tell him, you might be responsible for a murder. He's capable of that.

88

LARRY You the trumpet player?

THE MAN Yes.

LARRY You've got nothing to worry about: He thinks you're queer.

THE MAN He ought to consult his wife. (*To* HELEN) I'll call later.
        (*He exits.* LARRY *closes the door*)

LARRY Hubby goes to work and *you* play the piano to sound the all-clear. Clever.

HELEN What are you going to do?

LARRY I may never play again.

HELEN Do you think I care if you tell him?

LARRY No.

HELEN That's right. Not a bit and that's why you won't tell him. No one ever tries to hurt you when you don't care and I don't care about anything.

LARRY Including your son? (*No reply*) Well, don't you care about your son?

HELEN *Yes!* ... That make you happy.

LARRY   Suppose the kid found out you were playing around?

HELEN   He won't.

LARRY   Suppose he did? How would he feel?

HELEN   Are you going to preach?. . . If you're going to preach I'm going to walk out of this house and stay out till you're gone.

LARRY   If you and the Plowboy are so miserable together, split up. It would be easier on the kid.

HELEN   One more word and I'm walking out.

LARRY   I'm through.
        (*Begins to knot his tie*)

HELEN   I'm sorry you had to see all this.

LARRY   So am I.

HELEN   Can I get you more coffee?

LARRY   No thanks.
        (*Puts on his jacket*)

HELEN   You leaving?

LARRY Yes.

HELEN He'll wonder why you didn't wait.

LARRY Tell him my mother called. That she wasn't feeling well.

HELEN He'll only be a few minutes.

LARRY I couldn't face him right now. . . . Tell him I'll stop by tomorrow.

HELEN Tomorrow?

LARRY Yes. Sometime in the morning.

HELEN I thought you and your mother were leaving town this afternoon.

LARRY I changed my mind. We'll leave tomorrow instead.

HELEN Why?

LARRY I want to see the boy.

HELEN Why?

LARRY Because I want to.

HELEN But that's impossible. We don't know when he'll be home.

LARRY You said he'd be home tomorrow.

HELEN I mean we don't know what time. These relatives will be driving him down and we never know when they'll arrive. They have an old car and it's a long ride.

LARRY I'll wait.

HELEN It's possible they won't come till tomorrow night.

LARRY I'll wait.

HELEN Just to see the boy?

LARRY Yes.

HELEN You make it seem like the most important thing in the world.

LARRY (*Putting on his overcoat*) Tomorrow when the boy arrives, call me at the hotel. I'll come right up.

HELEN Suppose he doesn't arrive tomorrow.

LARRY I'll stay over. . . . I'm not leaving New York until I see him. (*Takes out a pad and pencil*) So there won't be any excuse for not calling, I'll leave the name of the hotel and my room number. (*Writes*) As far as me saying anything to the Plowboy about what happened this morning, you can rest easy. (*Finishes writing, offers her the paper*) Here. (HELEN *makes no move to accept the paper*)

HELEN   It's impossible to spare you if you won't spare yourself.

LARRY   What does that mean?

HELEN   That I beg you ... I beg you to leave this house without another word and never come back. Never come back. Never call. ... I beg you.

LARRY   Not until I see the boy.

HELEN   *There is no boy! ... There is no boy!*

LARRY   He's dead?

HELEN   That's what we tell people ... what we should have told you in the beginning. ... In my heart I know it's what I should tell you now, but I'm sick of lies. ... Just once I'd like to tell the truth about it.

LARRY   Go on ... go on.

HELEN   They have a complicated name for it ... a long medical word. ... What it means is ... What it means is I gave birth to a monster ... Yes. ... Not boy. Not girl. Not anything human ... not anything.

LARRY   He sent me a telegram when the baby was born. Said everything was fine and he was naming it after me.

HELEN   The hospital gave him the wrong report on the phone. When he got there they told him. They didn't tell *me* for a week. . . . I've never seen it. They put it some place. Some institution. We pay. I don't know where it is. . . . It took something in him and something in me. Something bad in the both of us to produce this thing. They say it couldn't happen again in fifty years. . . . You made it possible. . . . Again and again he'd tell that story. How he lay in the dark bleeding to death and heard the Lieutenant say, "Who'll save the Plowboy?" And then silence until you said, "I'll go." And each time I heard it my hate for you grew. . . . Why didn't you keep your mouth shut?

LARRY   He was my friend.

HELEN   He wasn't worth your pinky. He's a stupid, pitiful fool.

LARRY   Why did you marry him?

HELEN   It was the only offer I ever got. And he was the Plowboy then: strong, honest, kind. And there would be the farm. I'd never been to the country. He made it sound like paradise. Everyone said, "You'll never do any better and you could do lots worse." So I married him. And very soon I knew that I'd been swindled. . . . He was not strong. He was not honest. . . . He was not kind. . . .

94

LARRY Why don't you leave? Go away?

HELEN I did. . . . One day I got on a bus . . . was walking by the Greyhound terminal and just got on a bus. . . . Rode all across the country . . . passed all sorts of wonderful places . . . saw all sorts of beautiful sights. . . . But you know what? . . . It wasn't real to me . . . none of it . . . The only thing in the world that's real to me is here . . . this place . . . (*To* LARRY *directly*) Why did you do it? Why did you risk your life to save him?

LARRY I never thought why. I just did it.

HELEN I think about it all the time. I think what a fool you were. And how wrong. The best thing you could have done was let him die that night. He'd never admit it, but he feels that way himself.

LARRY No.

HELEN Yes. A plowboy who hates the country. He's lost in this world. He should have died that night. None of the others would try to save him. They all saw that it was impossible. . . . But you . . . you must do the impossible. And we all pay the penalty.

LARRY We *all* pay?

HELEN I meant he and I.

LARRY You said we all. You included me. How do *I* pay?
... *What do you know?*

HELEN Your mother was here.

LARRY She told you? (HELEN *nods*) Everything?

HELEN Yes.

LARRY She told the both of you?

HELEN Yes.

LARRY So that's why he was knocking himself out to be so
cheerful. . . . You should have heard the stories he told
me. . . . And that explains the tree.

HELEN I begged you to leave . . . I begged you.

LARRY It's my own fault. . . . Never should have come in the
first place. . . . Had this wild idea. . . . Was going to prove I
hadn't wasted my life. . . . Was going to find a nice family
and console myself that I was responsible for its existence. . . . Pretty wild, huh?

HELEN What will you do now?

LARRY Who knows. I may have to turn to God or whatever
you call it. . . . There's nothing else left. . . . When I was
young I was always vowing to get to the bottom of things.

The deepest level. I wanted to press my nose against it. I've done it now. . . . Looked at properly, maybe the whole thing has been a tremendous success.

HELEN   I hope so.

LARRY   Thanks. . . . You know we have accomplished one thing.

HELEN   What's that?

LARRY   You don't hate me any more. (*She takes his head in her hands, and gently kisses him; first on one cheek and then the other and then the forehead. For a moment they regard each other*) I think it's time for you to clean up your kitchen . . . time for me to go.

HELEN   Stay. Stay here. Let us care for you. We owe you that.

LARRY   Wouldn't work. I begrudge the Plowboy every breath he draws. When we got down to the wire I'd tell him so. . . . So long.
  (*He turns abruptly and goes toward the door as the door bell rings—three times long, two times short.* LARRY *halts*)

HELEN   It's Albert.

LARRY   Let him in.

97

HELEN   He couldn't have gone to the office and be back so soon.
   (*The ring is repeated*)

LARRY   Let him in.

HELEN   What are you going to say to him?

LARRY   I don't know.
   (*She goes to the door and admits* ALBERT *and a boy of eleven.* THE BOY *carries a gift-wrapped package*)

ALBERT (*Indicating* THE BOY)   Hi. Well say, will you look who I ran into as I stepped out of the house! (*To* THE BOY) Well, aren't you going to say hello to your mother? (THE BOY *hugs* HELEN, *who recoils from his touch*) That a boy. We stopped around the corner to get a present for Uncle Larry.

HELEN   You were supposed to go to the office.

ALBERT   I wanted to be here when the two Larrys met. (*To* THE BOY) Take your coat off.

HELEN   They'll fire you. They're just looking for a reason.

ALBERT   I don't give a damn. (*Goes to* LARRY) Hey, buddy, I got a surprise for you. He wasn't due back till tomorrow, but the folks wanted to do some shopping so they drove him down this morning. They were just dropping him off when I stepped out of the house.

98

LARRY *For Christ's sake, Plowboy!*

ALBERT What's the matter? . . . Oh, you mean about risking my job? Hell, buddy, don't give it a thought. Plenty of jobs around for an able man and I was pretty fed up with that one. (*Introducing* THE BOY *to* LARRY) Larry junior meet Larry senior. (LARRY *and* THE BOY *look at each other. To* THE BOY) Well, aren't you going to say something?

THE BOY Pleased to meet you.

ALBERT How about the present?
(THE BOY *extends the present to* LARRY)

THE BOY We bought this for you.
(LARRY *doesn't move to accept it*)

ALBERT Go on, buddy. It ain't no time bomb. Take it.
(LARRY *finally takes the package.* ALBERT *prompts* THE BOY)

THE BOY I always wanted to meet you . . . I heard a lot about you.

ALBERT (*To* LARRY, *indicating* THE BOY) What do you think of him? Most people say he takes after Helen. I can't see it myself. But at least he don't resemble me and that's something to be thankful for. Huh?

THE BOY (*Goes to the trains*) These the trains?

99

ALBERT That's right. (*To* LARRY) I told him about the trains. (*To* THE BOY) You like them? (THE BOY *nods yes. His attention is focused on the trains*) Well, what do you say to Uncle Larry?

THE BOY (*Without turning from the trains*) Thanks.

ALBERT (*To* LARRY) He's a little bit bashful.

THE BOY Make them run.

ALBERT Sure. (*Snaps on the switch and the trains begin to run. He turns to* LARRY) I told you he'd go for those trains. (*Notices now that* LARRY *is wearing his overcoat*) Hey, what have you got your coat on for?

LARRY I was just about to leave.

ALBERT Without saying good-by to me?

LARRY My mother called. They canceled our flight so we're taking an earlier one on another line.

ALBERT (*Stopping the trains*) Well, then I'm certainly glad I came home and you had a chance to meet young Larry. (*To* HELEN, *who has kept her back to him since* THE BOY's *entrance*) Hey, honey, Larry's going.

HELEN I know.

Rebecca Darke, William Smithers, Gerald O'Loughlin,
and Patrick O'Shaughnessy, as HELEN COBB, LARRY DOYLE,
ALBERT COBB, and THE BOY

ALBERT   Well come on, say good-by.

HELEN   We said our good-bys before you got here.

THE BOY   How do you make it go backwards?

ALBERT   Never mind that now. Uncle Larry is leaving.

THE BOY   You said it could go backwards.

ALBERT   It does. After Uncle Larry goes I'll show you. Now say good-by.

THE BOY   Bye.

ALBERT   (*Grabbing* THE BOY)   What kind of a good-by is that? Now you leave those trains alone and—

HELEN   (*Whirling*)   *Stop!*

ALBERT   But it's not right. He should have some manners.

LARRY   If he did, I wouldn't believe he was your son.
        (*The two men regard each other a moment, then* LARRY *smiles and* ALBERT *laughs*)

ALBERT   You son of a gun you. (*To* HELEN) That's the way he used to be all the time.

LARRY   If I'm going to make that plane I better get started. (*To* HELEN) Good-by again and good luck.

ALBERT   You've got our new address now, so there's no excuse for not writing.
(LARRY *goes to* THE BOY, *who is intent on the trains, and pats his head.* THE BOY *looks up, smiles*)

LARRY   Good-by, Larry.

THE BOY   Merry Christmas.

LARRY   Same to you.

ALBERT   I wouldn't be surprised if we came down to Florida on a vacation or something before too long.

LARRY   That'll be nice. (*Offers his hand to* ALBERT) So long, Plowboy.

ALBERT   So long, buddy. It's been great seeing you.

LARRY   Same here.

ALBERT   Take care of yourself.

LARRY   You too. (*To* HELEN *and* THE BOY) Bye.
(*He goes out.* ALBERT *follows him out into the hall and calls after him down the stairwell*)

ALBERT   Hey, buddy, I got a question for you.

LARRY (*From off stage*)   What's that?

ALBERT   Where's Santa Claus?

LARRY (*From off stage*)   He's lying down over in the corner
drunker than hell, but better than he was.

ALBERT (*Laughs loudly*)   Hey, buddy, wait till I get my coat,
I'll ride downtown with you . . . (*No answer*) Buddy? . . .
Buddy? (*No answer.* ALBERT *turns now and reënters the
apartment*) He's gone.

THE BOY   There's no tunnel.

ALBERT (*To* HELEN)   I think he believed it.

THE BOY   There's no station, either.

ALBERT (*To* THE BOY)   Go home.

THE BOY   Where's the box they came in?

ALBERT   Go home.

THE BOY   You said I could have the trains.

ALBERT   *Get out of here!*
        (*He approaches* THE BOY, *who, frightened, moves toward
        the door*)

THE BOY (*To* HELEN) He promised me the trains.

HELEN Come back tomorrow.

ALBERT He doesn't deserve them. He didn't say the things I told him to.

HELEN (*To* THE BOY) Come back tomorrow.

THE BOY What time?

HELEN Any time.

THE BOY All right.

HELEN What's your name?

THE BOY Joey . . . Joey Pike.

HELEN (*Takes a pencil and writes on the cover of the box the trains came in*) "Property of Joey Pike." There. (*She shows it to him*) Now you come back tomorrow.

THE BOY All right. (*He starts out, then turns to her*) Merry Christmas.
　　(*He exits*)

ALBERT I think Larry believed it. . . . The kid didn't say the things I told him to but I think he believed it anyway. . . . Maybe it was better that the kid didn't make such a fuss over him. It seemed more natural. . . . I was getting on the bus when I spotted this kid. From the side he looked a little like me. Like in those pictures on the farm when I was a kid. That's what gave me the idea. . . . It's gonna cost me my job but if he believes it, it's worth it. . . . Did you see the way he patted the kid on the head? . . . I think he believed it. . . . Don't you think he believed it?

HELEN Yes.

ALBERT I'm out of a job. I've got to make plans. I can't afford to get excited. (*The trumpet, extremely muted, is heard*) Well, it was worth it. . . . He believed me. . . . I owed him that. (*His eye is caught by the trains. He bends to them, turns a switch. The trains go backward*) I told him they went backwards.

Curtain

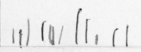